Helping Is Fun

written by Alice Greenspan

illustrated by Linda Hohag

Library of Congress Catalog Card No. 85-62952

© 1986. The STANDARD PUBLISHING Company, Cincinnati, Ohio
Division of STANDEX INTERNATIONAL Corporation. Printed in U.S.A.

Helping makes us happy.
It adds sunshine to our days.

And even though we're little,
we can help in many ways.

I can rake the leaves with Grandpa.

I can help Mother bake a pie.

I can put my socks and sneakers on.

I can hunt for Dad's brown tie.

I can climb up high on a bedroom chair,
and help Mother zip her dress.

I can bathe my little brown puppy,
when he's gotten in a mess.

I love to feed the goldfish,

and help clean the family car.

My dog and I run to get the mail,
 'long as Mother knows where we are.

I comb my hair,

and I brush my teeth.

I even shine Gramps old shoes.

I help watch my baby sister,
and if I tickle her, she coos.

I can use a nice clean tissue,
   when my nose begins to run.

I can water plants
and fold my pants,

because helping can be fun.

I love to pick blueberries,
  so Mother can make a dessert.

And I put my own little Band-Aid on,
when my knee begins to hurt.

I help my dad when he mows the yard,

then he hugs me extra hard.

And I know when I help others,
that I'm really helping God.